Children
of the
CIVIL WAR

Children
of the
CIVIL WAR

Candice F. Ransom

PICTURE
the
AMERICAN
PAST

Carolrhoda Books, Inc./Minneapolis

*For Ruth, fellow researcher and Fredericksburg writer.
And thanks to Janice Frye for her help.*

*Page one: Children and adults stand in front of boxes of supplies
ready to be sent to soldiers during the Civil War.*

*Page two: Free black children play in the ruins of a church in
Charleston, South Carolina, after war's end.*

*Opposite page: The Drum Corps and others gather in Momence,
Illinois, in 1864.*

Text copyright © 1998 by Candice F. Ransom

Carolrhoda Books, Inc., c/o The Lerner Publishing Group
241 First Avenue North, Minneapolis, MN 55401 U.S.A.

Website address: www.lernerbooks.com

LIBRARY OF CONGRESS CATALOGING-IN-PUBLICATION

Ransom, Candice F., 1952–
      Children of the Civil War / Candice F. Ransom.
          p.   cm. — (Picture the American past)
      Includes bibliographical references (p.   ) and index.
      Summary: Explores the lives of children during the Civil War, including those who
joined armies, others who stayed home, and the large numbers made homeless because of
the conflict.
      ISBN 1–57505–241–5
      1. United States—History—Civil War, 1861–1865—Children—Juvenile literature. [1.
United States—History—Civil War, 1861–1865.] I. Title. II. Series.
E468.9.R36 1998
973.7'083—dc21   97–32624

Manufactured in the United States of America
1 2 3 4 5 6 – JR – 03 02 01 00 99 98

CONTENTS

This family enjoys a game of croquet on the lawn of a plantation home.

Before the War

We cannot escape history.
—President Abraham Lincoln

In 1860, the Northern states and the Southern states were different worlds. The North had many cities. People had jobs in factories. The South was largely farmland. Big farms, called plantations, relied on slave labor.

Returning from the cotton fields in South Carolina in about 1860

The first slaves were brought to North America in 1619. They came from Africa and were forced to work in the New World.

By 1860, nearly four million slaves picked cotton, toiled in rice fields, or worked in plantation houses. Some slaves were blacksmiths who made farm tools and horseshoes. Others were fine cooks. Slave children also worked, feeding pigs, gathering eggs, and carrying water.

Slaves escape into the night.

Slaves often ran away. If they could, they tried to make it to the North. There, the laws were different and slaves were free. But running away was dangerous. Many slaves were injured or killed trying to escape.

Like farm animals, slaves were property. They had no rights. Families could be separated and sold to different farms. Slaves were not allowed to read or write. Their children could not go to school.

Slavery was a hot issue in 1860. Northern states wanted to end it. Southern states didn't agree. They didn't believe Northerners should make laws that affected the South.

The United States of America, also called the Union, split in half. One by one, Southern states broke away. They formed a new country—the Confederate States of America.

Northerners would not let the South leave the Union. All the states must stay together, they said. A divided country was weak. In April 1861, the first shot was fired.

The war began.

A Southern black family poses for the camera.

Above: Cadet Thomas Garland Jefferson
Opposite page: Drum and Fife Corps, 93rd New York Infantry. Two of these boys were 15 and 16 years old.

A War-Torn Land

I am determined to go to war.
—fourteen-year-old boy who followed
the troops on his mule

Many in both the North and the South were eager to fight. Men rushed to join the army. Boys did, too. At least three hundred Northern soldiers were 13 years old or younger. These boys played music as drummers or buglers. Some carried messages from one camp to another.

Johnny Clem was small enough to fit in a drum.

Johnny Clem was a famous drummer boy. He joined the Union army at age 11. In Tennessee, a cannon shell destroyed his drum. Johnny picked up a musket and began shooting. He was later promoted to sergeant and given a silver medal.

A black drummer boy from the United States Colored Infantry

African-American boys also beat the long drumroll. This young man stands tall in his uniform.

A servant to an army officer

Other African-Americans served officers in camp. For these boys, wartime meant fixing meals. It meant washing dishes and moving camp whenever the lines of battle changed.

Boys at the Virginia Military Institute studied to be soldiers. Drilling and marching were fine, but the boys longed to fight. In May 1864, VMI cadets were called into battle. Real fighting was hard and scary, as they soon found out. The mud was so deep, the boys lost their shoes. Ten young cadets died in battle or from wounds. The field where they died is called the Field of Lost Shoes.

The field that became the Field of Lost Shoes. Thomas Garland Jefferson (pictured on page 12) died from his wounds three days after the battle here.

Rose Greenhow and "Little Rose." Mrs. Greenhow's daughter became ill in prison without proper food and fresh air. After six months, both were allowed to go free.

Women and girls took part in the war, too. Some dressed as men and became soldiers. Others became spies.

Confederate spy Rose Greenhow passed maps and coded messages. She was captured and sent to prison in Washington, D.C. Her eight-year-old daughter, also named Rose, went to jail with her. Mrs. Greenhow's letters and books were searched for secret messages. Even young Rose's scribbles were studied for secrets.

A family washes clothes and cooks in the camp of the 31st Pennsylvania Infantry near Washington, D.C.

Some families followed the war. With husbands away, women had trouble running farms alone. So they "joined" the army. They brought their children, their belongings, and their dogs. They slept in tents or under the stars. When the army moved to a new place, families marched with the troops.

In Springfield, Illinois, Northern women put together packages for soldiers.

Nearly everyone helped with the war effort. Girls rolled bandages for injured soldiers. They also sent boxes of soap, writing paper, and facecloths to the boys in the blue uniforms of the North or the boys in the gray uniforms of the South.

A Southern farm family sits and sews outdoors.

After battles, railway lines and roads were often blocked. People were cut off from supplies. Ordinary items became hard to buy. Women and girls learned to make dresses, shirts, coats, and even shoes.

This young woman writes a letter for a wounded soldier.

Girls wrote letters to their brothers and fathers. They also kept diaries. Many of these journals have survived. These records let us see the war through the eyes of a young girl.

"There was firing, fighting, and bringing in the wounded all that day," wrote Sue Chancellor. When she was 14, the Battle of Chancellorsville surrounded her family's house in Virginia.

Sue and her family barely escaped. "The woods around the house were a sheet of fire...," she wrote later. "At our last look, our old home was completely enveloped in flames."

These children watch soldiers cross a creek, not far from the site of the second Battle of Bull Run in Virginia.

Early in the war, children from the North waved when trains carried soldiers through their towns. Southern children became used to the sight of armies marching down country roads.

War soon became a way of life. Most of the battles occurred on Southern soil. Children explored battlefields after the fighting. Boys searched for souvenirs—canteens, hats, belt buckles. A real prize was a battle flag.

Life wasn't all fighting. In Northern cities and Southern towns, there were parades and rallies to raise money for the troops. Bands played stirring music and crowds cheered.

Even in towns far from battlefields, no one could forget the war. And in battle-scarred places, music was a welcome relief.

Schoolchildren welcome the army parading in Washington, D.C.

A black family listens as a Union soldier reads the Emancipation Proclamation.

The war dragged on. Southern black families waited for the war to end. They hoped for freedom.

On New Year's Day, 1863, President Lincoln issued an order to free the slaves in the rebelling states. This order was called the Emancipation Proclamation.

A black family flees from battle, their belongings piled on an ox-drawn wagon.

After the Emancipation Proclamation, some black families were homeless. Some went to live near Northern troops. Others continued to live and work on plantations. Many slave owners didn't tell their workers that they were free.

War damages everything it touches. Families trapped in the path of battle usually lost. They lost their homes, their crops, even their lives. Some families fled, chased by war. They left their houses before troops clashed on their land.

These white faces are grim. These people are running from advancing armies.

A family in Baton Rouge, Louisiana, looks through what is left of its home.

Many beautiful Southern homes were destroyed. Artillery fire and mortar shells leveled houses. Angry enemy troops often burned down fine old homes.

Some families went to live with relatives in another town. Some stayed, camping out nearby. One woman moved her children into a cave.

Finding food was a real problem. Armies on both sides raided farms to steal cows, pigs, and chickens for soldiers and grain for their horses. Women and children hunted for food. Often they went to bed hungry.

Children in the Southern states often couldn't go to school. Schools were used as hospitals for wounded soldiers. The buildings were also bombed during battle or burned by the enemy. Businesses, mills, roads, and railroads were not spared either. By destroying Southern property, Union troops hoped to end the war quickly.

Union troops burned the Virginia Military Institute. Even the books in the library were destroyed.

A Union officer has moved into this North Carolina home with his own family.

Not all houses were ruined. Officers from both armies took over homes to use as their headquarters.

And not all families fled, not even during the heat of battle. Some families had no place to go. If they ran away, they couldn't protect their property. When the war ended, they would need a home. So they stayed in their houses, facing the dangers of war.

The children of Confederate president Jefferson Davis pose for a photographer. They stayed in the Confederate capital, Richmond, Virginia, until the last days of the war.

The McLean house at Appomattox Court House, Virginia, where Lee and Grant met. In the parlor, General Grant accepted the surrender of General Lee's army.

After the War

Childhood had slipped away from me,
never to return.
—From the diary of Celine Fremaux,
a Louisiana girl

No one thought the war would last so long. Both sides believed the enemy could be "whipped" in a few weeks.

On April 9, 1865, General Robert E. Lee of the Confederacy surrendered his army to Ulysses S. Grant, commander of the Union forces. After four years of fighting, the war was over.

Homecomings were times of celebration. Husbands, fathers, brothers, and sons went home to their families.

Most Southern soldiers returned to their farms. They took up the plow and life went on. Northern soldiers went back to factory jobs. Everyone was glad to be home.

Returning black soldiers meet their families.

A soldier who lost a leg visits the headquarters of the U.S. Christian Commission in Washington, D.C.

But many men had been wounded. Some stayed in hospitals for months. The lucky ones still had both arms and legs. It was hard for a farmer to work the land with one leg. It was hard for a factory worker to run a machine if he was blind.

This photograph was found in the hand of a dead soldier after the Battle of Gettysburg, Pennsylvania. This picture was widely published. Songs were written about the "Children of the Battlefield."

Some brothers and fathers did not come home. Nearly 625,000 men and boys died from injuries and disease during the war. Children who had helped their mothers during the war had to carry on that job.

The littlest victims were children. Many were orphaned. Their fathers were killed. Their mothers died of illness. These children had no place to go but orphans' homes.

Money from the sale of the "Children of the Battlefield" photograph and songs helped build this orphanage at Gettysburg.

Some good things came after the war. Before, slaves had not been allowed to learn to read or write. With the end of slavery, black children could go to school in the South for the first time.

A former slave, Charles Whiteside, thought this was a wonderful thing. "Education," he said, "was the next best thing to liberty."

African-American children pose in front of their school in South Carolina.

After the war has ended, people attend the dedication of a monument to the dead in the first Battle of Bull Run.

People were anxious to heal the wounds of war. But they did not want to bury the past.

Americans would never forget the terrible conflict that tore the nation apart. Children planted flowers on soldiers' graves. They watched as monuments were built on land that was once the site of fierce fighting.

After the war, soldiers from both sides met on the battlefields where they had fought. This time they shook hands.

CIVIL WAR MESSAGES

Instructions for a Secret Code Wheel

During the Civil War, it was important to get information through battle lines. Enemy territory—whether won in that day's fighting or long fallen to the winning army—was heavily patrolled. Guards stopped any stranger who might be a spy. Spies tried to learn the other army's secrets, such as the number of horses, and report back to their side. They often used codes to send this information. If the spy was captured, the enemy could not read the message. One way to keep messages secret was to use a code wheel.

SECRET CODE WHEEL

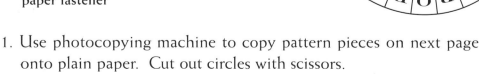

access to a photocopying machine

scissors

lightweight cardboard or construction paper

pencil

glue stick

pushpin

paper fastener

1. Use photocopying machine to copy pattern pieces on next page onto plain paper. Cut out circles with scissors.

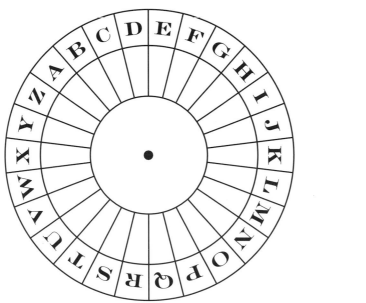
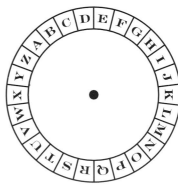

2. While holding paper circles in place on top of lightweight cardboard or construction paper, trace around each one. Cut out circle shapes.

3. Use glue stick to spread glue onto cardboard circles. Making sure that the letters are facing up, lay paper circles over cardboard circles. Press to seal. Trim any excess cardboard.

4. Use pushpin to make a small hole through the dot in the center of each circle. Push the point of a pencil partway through the circles to enlarge each hole.

5. Thread paper fastener first through smaller circle and then through larger one. Press paper fastener ends to hold the two circles together. You should be able to move wheels easily.

6. To write a message, first choose a letter. This will be your key letter. It could be the first letter in your first name. Just make sure it's something easy to remember and make sure it isn't the letter *A*. Find your key letter on the large wheel. Turn the small wheel until the letter *A* is opposite your key letter.
Decide what your message will be. Then, for each letter in your message, find the letter on the smaller wheel. Copy down the letter opposite that letter on the larger wheel. Once your coded message is complete, send it to a friend. Have your friend send you a secret message!

7. To decode a message, you must know your friend's key letter. (And your friend must know yours.) Find the key letter on the larger wheel. Line up the key letter with the letter *A* on the smaller wheel. Do not move the wheels.
Match each letter in the message with a letter on the large wheel. Then write down the opposite letter from the small wheel. This will be the real message! Try sending this sample message: *Meet me after school.*

NOTE TO TEACHERS AND ADULTS

For children, Civil War times may seem like part of a far-off past. But there are many ways to make this era and its people come alive. Along with helping children make a wheel for decoding secret messages, you can explore America's Civil War past in other ways. One way is to read more about the war, and more books on the topic are listed on pages 45 and 46. Another way to explore the past is to train young readers to study historical photographs. Historical photographs hold many clues about how life was lived in earlier times.

Ask your children or students to look for the details and "read" all the information in each picture in this book. For example, how do the clothes worn by girls in the photos on pages 1, 6, 18, 19, and 31 differ from clothes worn by girls today? And why are so many of the boys shown in this book wearing caps? (For those in the army, a cap was part of the uniform. Boys living at home commonly wore felt or leather caps.)

To better learn to read historical photographs, have young readers try these activities:

On the Move
Study the photos on pages 26 and 27 of children and families on the move during the Civil War. How are these people moving? What are they carrying with them? Based on what you have read, can you make an educated guess about why they are moving? What clues can you find in the photographs that suggest a war is going on? Next, think about a time when you moved and draw a picture of your move. (If you have never moved, ask a friend or family member to describe moving.) How did you travel? What did you take with you? Why did you have to move? Add details to your

picture that help to answer these questions. Then ask a classmate or family member to study your drawing and try to answer the questions above.

Writing Letters

During the war, people couldn't communicate with family and friends by telephone or E-mail—neither had been invented yet. Letters to family *from* soldiers brought details of what life was like in battle or in camp. Letters *to* soldiers from home carried all the latest news of family and friends. Pick one of the children shown in the photographs in this book. Then write a letter from that child's point of view, or perspective. If you are writing from the perspective of a soldier, drummer boy, or camp servant (see pages 12 through 16), describe your life in the army for family and friends back home. What do you miss the most? How do you spend your days? If you are writing from the perspective of a child not in the army, describe how your life has changed due to war. Have you had to move? Is it hard to buy clothes or find food? Have battles taken place near your home?

Growing Up in Civil War Times

Dress in costume and tell your friends, parents, or classmates what it was like to grow up during the Civil War. Read the text—and the photos—in this book for information and details about daily life. To add to your presentation, read some of the books about the Civil War on pages 45 and 46. If you are playing the part of a drummer boy, like Johnny Clem, or of another boy who served in the army, take a look at *The Boys' War: Confederate and Union Soldiers Talk About the Civil War.* For several different perspectives on the war, read *Bull Run,* a novel about the war's first major battle.

RESOURCES ON THE CIVIL WAR

Armstrong, Jennifer. *The Dreams of Mairhe Mehan: A Novel of the Civil War.* New York: Alfred A. Knopf, 1996. Haunting and harsh, this novel for older readers follows the story of a young immigrant who lives in Washington, D.C.'s, Irish slum and whose beloved brother, Mike, has joined the Union army.

Bolotin, Norman and Angela Herb. *For Home and Country: A Civil War Scrapbook.* New York: Lodestar Books, 1995. Part of a series of books covering the history of the war, this volume is packed with pictures, letters, and stories of the war years.

Channing, Steven A., and the editors of Time-Life Books. *Confederate Ordeal: The Southern Home Front.* Alexandria, Va.: Time-Life Books, 1984. This amply illustrated book for older readers looks at home life in the South, where most Civil War battles were fought.

Damon, Duane. *When This Cruel War Is Over: The Civil War Homefront.* Minneapolis, Minn.: Lerner Publications Company, 1996. Damon tells the story of civilians— the boys and girls who helped run family farms, the nurses who helped the sick, and the factory workers who made shells and guns.

Donahue, John. *An Island Far from Home.* Minneapolis, Minn.: Carolrhoda Books, 1995. Twelve-year-old Joshua Loring lives in small-town Massachusetts and yearns to join the Union army. Through his uncle, an army doctor, and a classroom letter-writing assignment, he instead ends up befriending a Confederate soldier, Private John Meadows.

Fleischman, Paul. *Bull Run*. New York: A Laura Geringer Book, HarperCollins Publishers, 1993. The story of the first Battle of Bull Run in 1861 is told through alternating voices of a cast of characters, from a general to a fife player to a slave girl.

Hakim, Joy. *War, Terrible War*. New York: Oxford University Press, 1994. Part of a series of books covering the history of the United States, this volume focuses on the years 1861 to 1865, when the Civil War was fought.

Murphy, Jim. *The Boys' War: Confederate and Union Soldiers Talk About the Civil War*. New York: Clarion Books, 1990. Using first-hand accounts from boys who served in the Confederate and Union armies, Murphy shows the horrors of war, the boredom of army life, and the warmth of friendships forged between soldiers of all ages.

Polacco, Patricia. Illustrations by the author. *Pink and Say*. New York: Philomel Books, 1994. In this picture storybook, two boys, Sheldon "Say" Russell Curtis and Pinkus "Pink" Aylee, must find their way back to their outfits in the Union army after a fierce battle leaves one of them wounded and both of them lost behind Confederate lines.

Websites about the Civil War

http://www.nps.gov/gett/
The official Website of Gettysburg National Military Park in Pennsylvania contains photographs and information on the battle and on daily life for soldiers.

http://lcweb2.loc.gov/ammem/cwphome
Part of American Memory, a project devoted to putting historical images online, this Website contains many photographs taken during the Civil War.

New Words

Civil War: a war fought among the states in the United States of America from 1861 to 1865. This is often called the war of "brother against brother."
Confederate States of America: the states that left the United States. These Southern states formed their own country.
plantations: large farms in the Southern United States. These farms were worked by slaves who lived there.
slavery: forcing people to work. A slave is a person owned by another person.
Union: the Northern states at the time of the Civil War. After Southern states left to form the Confederate States of America, the remaining United States were known as the Union.

Index

TIME LINE

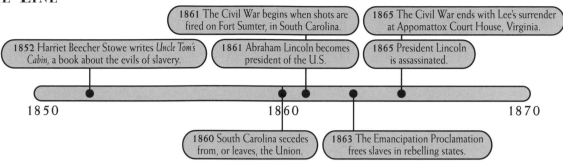

1861 The Civil War begins when shots are fired on Fort Sumter, in South Carolina.

1865 The Civil War ends with Lee's surrender at Appomattox Court House, Virginia.

1852 Harriet Beecher Stowe writes *Uncle Tom's Cabin*, a book about the evils of slavery.

1861 Abraham Lincoln becomes president of the U.S.

1865 President Lincoln is assassinated.

1850   1860   1870

1860 South Carolina secedes from, or leaves, the Union.

1863 The Emancipation Proclamation frees slaves in rebelling states.

ABOUT THE AUTHOR

Candice F. Ransom grew up in Manassas and Centreville, Virginia. Manassas was the site of two famous battles. Soldiers camped out or fought small battles around Centreville. Often bullets or canteens were found in the woods or garden where Ms. Ransom lived. Now she and her husband, Frank, live in Fredericksburg, Virginia. Five major battles were fought in and around the city. Behind their house is an old railroad track. It once transported slaves and is now protected land.

Ms. Ransom is the author of several Carolrhoda books, including *Fire in the Sky*, a story about the crash of the *Hindenburg*, and *Jimmy Crack Corn*, a story set during the Great Depression.

PHOTO ACKNOWLEDGMENTS

The photographs in this book are reproduced through the courtesy of: The Library of Congress, front cover, back cover, pp. 2, 6, 7, 9, 10, 13, 14, 18, 19, 21, 23, 24, 25, 26, 31, 34, 35; Corbis-Bettmann, p. 1; Chicago Historical Society, pp. 5, 20; Collection of the New-York Historical Society, p. 8; Virginia Military Institute Archives, pp. 12, 29; National Archives, pp. 15 (IG5-JT-302), 16 (111-B-247), 27 (Gift Collection, 200-CC-306), 32 (W&C 259), 33 (165-SB-100), 39 (165-SB-100); Virginia Military Institute Museum, p. 17; Massachusetts Commandery, Military Order of the Loyal Legion and the U.S. Army Military Institute, pp. 22, 38; Andrew D. Lytle Collection, Louisiana and Lower Mississippi Valley Collections, LSU Libraries, Louisiana State University, p. 28; Society for the Preservation of New England Antiquities, neg. no. 11372-B, p. 30; The J. Howard Wert Gettysburg Collection, p. 36; William J. Little Collection, U.S. Army Military History Institute, p. 37; Steve Schweitzer, pp. 40, 41.

j973.7   Ransom, Candice F.
RAN   Children of the Civil
          War

$22.60

DATE